Contents

The Magic Pot

A Traditional Tale

Illustrated by Ellen Giggenbach

There was once a young girl
who lived with her mother
in a little house.
They were very poor.
They were often very hungry.

One day, an old woman saw the girl.
She could see the girl was hungry,
and she felt sorry for her.
The old woman gave the girl
a magic pot.

3

She said to the girl,
"Say, 'Cook, little pot, cook',
and the magic pot
will cook you porridge.
When you have enough porridge,
say, 'Stop, little pot, stop',
and the magic pot will stop cooking."

The girl took the magic pot to her mother.
She said, "Cook, little pot, cook,"
and the pot filled with porridge.
The girl and her mother ate all they wanted.

Then the girl said,
"Stop, little pot, stop,"
and the magic pot stopped cooking.

One day, the girl went out.
Her mother was hungry,
so she said, "Cook, little pot, cook."

The magic pot filled with porridge.
The mother ate all she wanted,
then she said, "No more, little pot."

But the pot still cooked and cooked.
The mother could not think
of the words to stop the pot cooking.

When the girl came back,
there was porridge
all over the table,
all over the floor,
and running out the door.

Make a Cake House

You will need:

1. Cut the corners to make the roof.

2. Spread on the icing.

3. Put on the door, roof, and windows.

4. Decorate your cake house.

9

Chocolate Cake

Chocolate cake,
chocolate cake,
that's the one
I'll help you make.

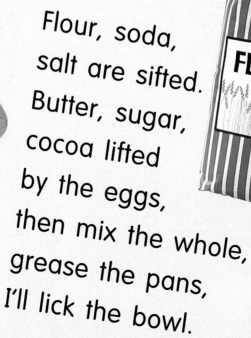

Flour, soda,
salt are sifted.
Butter, sugar,
cocoa lifted
by the eggs,
then mix the whole,
grease the pans,
I'll lick the bowl.

At once, the girl cried, "Stop, little pot, stop!"
and the magic pot stopped cooking.

But the girl and her mother stepped
in sticky porridge for days and days!

That Takes the Cake

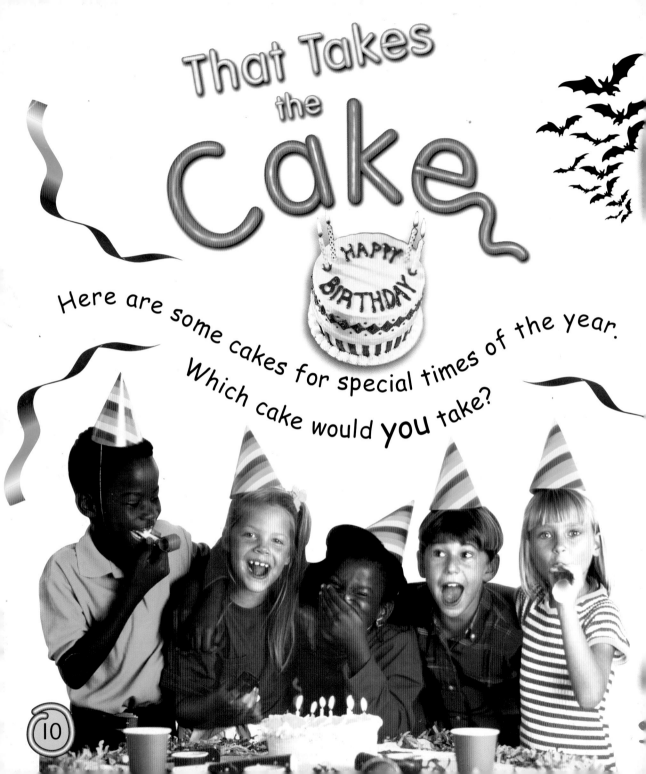

Here are some cakes for special times of the year. Which cake would **you** take?

Chocolate caked,
chocolate caked,
that's what I'll be
when it's baked.

Nina Payne

Crossword

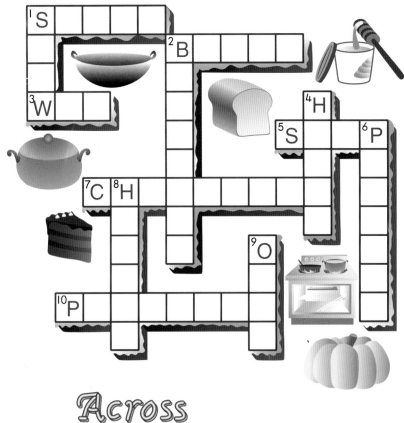

Down

1. Mr. Winkle cooked this. (p.14)
2. People use this when they cook outside. (p.30)
4. Emily puts this on her sandwich. (p.39)
6. Mum will cook this tonight. (p.40)
8. The girl looked... so the old lady gave her the magic pot. (p.2)
9. Pizza is cooked in one of these. (p.32)

Across

1. You need this to make a chocolate cake. (p.8)
2. You need this to make a sandwich. (p.35)
3. Many Asian meals are cooked in this. (p.33)
5. This meal was made from a stone. (p.44)
7. This is the kind of cake I'll help you make. (p.8)
10. The magic pot cooked this. (p.4)

Halloween cake

Chinese moon cake

Easter cake

Christmas gingerbread cake

11

The Big, Brown Pot

Written by Margaret Mahy   Illustrated by Helen Bacon

One day, Mr. Winkle made
a wonderful stew in his big, brown pot.

14

The stew smelled so delicious
that Mr. Winkle said to himself,
"This stew is too good for one person.
I shall go and visit *my* friend, Tom,
and take this stew with me."

15

So Mr. Winkle went out to his car.
He put the big, brown pot of stew
on the roof of the car
while he opened the door.
Then he got in and drove away.

BUT Mr. Winkle left the big, brown pot
of stew on the roof of his car.

17

Brown Dog and White Dog
were out in the street.
They sniffed the stew
as Mr. Winkle drove by.
It smelled wonderful.

Brown Dog ran after the car,
and White Dog ran after Brown Dog.

18

The dog-catcher saw
Brown Dog and White Dog
chasing Mr. Winkle's car.

Off went the dog-catcher
following White Dog,
who was following Brown Dog,
who was following the stew,
which was in the big, brown pot,
which was on the roof of Mr. Winkle's car.

19

Mrs. Bright looked out of the window
and saw the dog-catcher following the dogs.
"Those are *my* dogs!" she cried.
"I *must* tell the dog-catcher."

20

Mrs. Bright put on her helmet.
She climbed on her motorbike,
and off she went,
following the dog-catcher,
who was following White Dog,
who was following Brown Dog,
who was following the stew,
which was in the big, brown pot,
which was on the roof of Mr. Winkle's car.

21

The police were driving by in their police car.

"What's going on over there?" they said.

"We'd better find out."

So they followed Mrs. Bright,
who was following the dog-catcher,
who was following White Dog,
who was following Brown Dog,
who was following the stew,
which was in the big, brown pot,
which was on the roof of Mr. Winkle's car.

23

Inside the car, Mr. Winkle suddenly thought,
"But today's Friday. Tom will be at work.
Oh dear, I'd better go home.
Oh dear, oh dear, no one to share
my beautiful stew."

Off he drove, around the park,
followed by Brown Dog,
who was followed by White Dog,
who was followed by the dog-catcher,
who was followed by Mrs. Bright,
who was followed by the police.
He drove all the way home
and stopped outside his own gate.

Up came Brown Dog and White Dog.
Up came the dog-catcher in his van.
Up came Mrs. Bright on her motorbike.
Up came the police in their car.

Mr. Winkle was looking for the stew.
It wasn't on the front seat or the back seat.
"It's gone," he cried. "My big, brown pot
of delicious stew has gone!"

26

Everyone pointed and shouted.
"Look, Mr. Winkle.
Look on the roof of your car!"

"There it is," cried Mr. Winkle.
"My beautiful pot! My beautiful stew!
Is anybody hungry?" he said.

"We all are," they cried.

"Then come inside and share *my* stew.
There is plenty for all in *my* big, brown pot!"

27

What's Cooking?

Fried

Baked

Roasted

All around the world, people cook food in different ways. Food can be baked, fried, roasted, steamed, grilled, and boiled.

Steamed

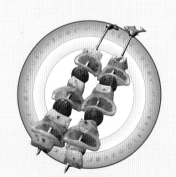

Grilled

Boiled

29

Long ago, people cooked
their food over a fire.
Today, people in many
parts of the world
use a barbecue
to cook this way.

In New Zealand and the Pacific Islands, people sometimes cook food in earth ovens. The food is wrapped and then put on top of hot stones. The heat and steam cook the food.

In India, some people cook their food in a tandoor, which is an oven made from clay and shaped like a giant pot.

31

In Turkey, some people cook their meat on a spit. As the spit slowly turns, the meat is roasted.

In Italy, people put their favourite toppings on flat, round dough and cook it in a pizza oven.

In China and other Asian countries, people often cook their food in a wok. The shape of the wok helps the food cook quickly.

So what's cooking in your part of the world tonight?

A Matter of Taste

Written by Pip Harrison   Illustrated by Christine Ross

"Hi, Mum," called Emily,
as she came in from school.
"I'm hungry!"

Mum was upstairs.
"Make yourself a sandwich, Emily.
I'll be down in a minute."

34

Emily opened the cupboard.
She got the peanut butter,
the honey, and the chocolate chips.
She took out the bread,
two knives, and two plates.

Then Emily's brother, Scott, came in.
He opened the fridge.
He took out the butter,
some ham, and the tomato sauce.

36

"Good idea, Scott," said Emily.
They buttered their bread.
They put on their toppings.

Mum came downstairs.
"How was school?" she asked.
Then she saw their sandwiches.
"What ARE you making?"

The children put the top pieces of bread on their sandwiches.

Scott bit into his ham, tomato sauce, and chocolate chip sandwich.
"Yum!" he said.

Emily bit into her ham,
peanut butter, and honey sandwich.
"Delicious!" she said.
"Do you want one, Mum?"

"Ummm, no thanks, Emily," said Mum.
"I think I'll have something else."
She made herself a cup of coffee
and buttered a cracker.

"What's for dinner, Mum?" asked Scott.

"I'd like to try something new," said Mum.
"This sounds delicious. I need some
chicken, some orange juice, some pumpkin,
some onion, some herbs, and some nuts.
I'll cook some peas to go with it!"

40

Emily and Scott looked at each other.
"Mum…," they said, "can we have another
sandwich instead?"

Stone Soup

A Traditional Story

Illustrated by Yukari Kakita

Characters

Narrator

Woman

Man

Boy

Girl

 Narrator: There was once a man who made friends wherever he went.

Man: How hungry I am. Maybe the people who live here will share a meal with me.

Narrator: Knock, knock, knock!

 Woman: What do you want?

 Man: Good day, kind woman.
I have walked a long way
and I am hungry. Would you
let me share a meal with you?

 Woman: I'm sorry, sir.
We have enough food for ourselves,
but we have nothing left to share.

 Man: Well, let me help you.
I have a stone.
With it, I'll make stone soup.

Girl: Stone soup! I've never seen soup made from a stone.

 Man: Why don't you let me in and bring me a pot of water. I'll make stone soup for you.

 Woman: Ha, ha, ha! You can't make soup from a stone.

 Boy: Is it good soup?

 Man: Stone soup is fit for a king.

 Narrator: The woman brought the man a pot of water. He put the stone into the pot and stirred.

47

Man: I've used this stone many times. The soup may need some rice to make it good and thick.

 Woman: I'll get some rice for you.

 Narrator: The man added the rice to the soup.

 Man: Mmm... a little meat, I think.

 Boy: I'll get some meat for you.

 Man: Thanks! Now carrots and peas would make it the best soup.

 Girl: I'll get some from the garden.

49

Narrator: The man tasted the soup.

 Man: The soup is ready. Let's eat!

 Girl: How delicious this soup is.

 Boy: And all made from a stone!

 Woman: Thank you, friend. That was a happy meal we shared.

 Man: The stone is yours. Farewell!

 Narrator: As the man walked away, he picked up a new stone and put it in his pocket.

51

Letters That Go Together

ch chocolate   **wh** which, who

Words That Go Together

herself   maybe

himself   yourself

Describing Words I Know

beautiful

delicious

wonderful

Words I Know

after	hungry	saw	which
another	often	still	while
enough	once	wanted	who
how	over	was	wonderful

52